DON'TS

FOR DEANS & ACADEMIC
LEADERS

DON'TS
FOR DEANS & ACADEMIC LEADERS

A HIGHER EDUCATION GUIDEBOOK

MICHAEL STEPNIAK

atmosphere press

PREFACE

Dear Reader,

This guidebook is offered as a practical aid, an aid to help you
– as a new or aspiring chair, director, dean, or provost – avoid
learning lessons through painful experience. It is written with
the assumption that you are already familiar with (or striving
to become familiar with) the many significant trends impacting higher education. Consequently, it pays little attention to
such issues as AI's role in learning and teaching, the decline
in the humanities, the rise of non-traditional learners, the
development of non-tuition revenue, and the implications of
laws passed by state legislatures targeting campus culture and
governance. A plethora of well-written articles continue to
address these and similar issues. This volume deals, instead,
with the messier business of leading, of building and maintaining those relationships that support effective leadership.

The offered list of terms and concepts is, as you will quickly
note, preoccupied with faculty. The reason for this is straightforward: relationships with faculty, as many higher education
academic leaders quickly find, eclipse all other areas in terms
of complexity and import. Faculty are somewhere between
gladiators and a mob. And I, like so many other academic
leaders, have gotten to know them in either state.

An additional acknowledgment. This guidebook was orig-
inally inspired by, and at times builds directly on, Blanche
Ebbutt's quaint pocket books, *Don'ts for Husbands* and *Don'ts
for Wives*. ("Don't" statements so linked are identified in the
book by an asterisk.) There are, it turns out, surprising paral-
lels between the work of maintaining a marriage relationship,

however defined, and of being an effective and trusted higher education academic leader.

Beyond being immodestly humanistic in orientation and origin, this guidebook is also inspired by a range of leadership scholars and the wit and whimsy occasionally found in such works as Ambrose Bierce's *The Devil's Dictionary* and Gustave Flaubert's *Dictionary of Platitudes*. Humor, in the end, is one of the most valuable companions for any academic leader.

Finally, a word of appreciation and thanks. This book builds on many practical lessons learned and still being learned from mentors and friends. Those include (especially) Barbara Kellerman, Dick Chait, Randy Boxx, Tracy Fitzsimmons, Hakeem Leonard and the many faculty and staff I've been privileged to support and even, occasionally, lead. I am indebted to them all.

Michael Stepniak
Winchester, Virginia

****

ACTIONS

Don't over-attribute results to your actions. Do everything as if it matters. You can't truly know what works or will make a difference.

This doesn't mean micromanaging or constantly turning to tinker with project details. It means ensuring that what you do is done with care. If you make excellence and care your goal for all that you do – from overseeing an agenda to supporting faculty and staff in a major project – you will better ensure initiatives have a chance for success. Beyond that, you will be modeling integrity, something which will help strengthen your community's vitality and bolster a culture that is better able to attract and support exceptionally talented faculty and staff. (See, also, "Expectations.")

ALUMNI

Don't neglect to keep them informed and updated. If you do keep them informed, your school or department will be more often rewarded with individuals who suddenly appear ready and interested to engage with and even invest in their alma mater.

As advancement professionals know, virtually all alumni giving emerges from within nurtured relationships. This has several practical implications. You definitely should take the time to attend all alumni events. You should ask program directors to keep you informed of any alumni news they hear. And you should set a Google search alert for your school. Following up on news – whether promotions, hiring, or passing – is one of the simplest and, because it's so personal, most powerful ways to build the relationship between your alumni (and their spouses/families) and your school. Yes, you will need to be prudent with your time, but don't ignore those alumni with lower capacity to give. Treat all with gratitude and respect.

ARTISTS & THE ARTS

Don't diminish opportunities for artists and the arts to be visible in your school. They can greatly vitalize spaces and communities. Karen Armstrong was right: art enables us to see our world from a perspective that goes beyond our own self-interest.

There's a reason that larger public universities strong in sciences or technology have increasingly invested in building new arts buildings and programs: such additions help attract creative (and energetic) students to campus and, not infrequently, wealthy donors. There is new vitality when visual and performing artists add to an institution's weekly programming, and when the handiwork of visual artists, whether student or professional, begins to fill buildings. Any building that is alive with the arts is, by definition, the opposite of sterile. At their core, the arts are works in process, endeavors that are fully alive with inquiry, passion and exploration. A Māori whakataukī (proverb) puts it differently: where there is artistic excellence, there is human dignity. When present on campuses, artists and artworks are both seen and felt.

ASSESSMENT

Don't fail to delegate, and celebrate champions of it where you have them. Formal assessment always holds great promise. Unfortunately, it is typically the plaything of bureaucrats. Sporting jargon-filled language, assessment never fails to support reductionist thinking, to beguile those who have a soft spot for rules and regulations, and to dispirit many faculty.

If you are a dean or department chair who relishes the work of assessment, you are of a wonderful and rare breed. More likely, you are in a position where you must ensure the presence of broad and deep assessment even while you empathize with many faculty who find it tedious at best. To support your people and this necessary process, consistently affirm that assessment is primarily the evaluation of how well programs and units are supporting the faculty's most important goals and values. Yes, a good deal of assessment will be dictated, and concerning issues that might be of less importance to faculty or programs. But if you continually highlight the ways assessment can be useful and meaningful to programs and units while acknowledging that there will be some drudgery, you will advance collective work in this area.

ATTITUDE

Don't talk down to your faculty; those around you may well be smarter than you. A generous attitude is often more important than facts, and will rarely be resented.

It doesn't take much living within academia to notice that what information is shared is typically secondary in import to how it is shared. Whether in meetings with faculty or fellow academic leaders, a spirit of generosity and true inquiry is the best guarantor of engagement by others. Faculty are typically highly focused on their own priorities. As specialists in their individual disciplinary fields, they are accustomed to expecting respect, starting with but extending (rightly or wrongly) far beyond their field of expertise. To put it differently, faculty and fellow administrators, even more than the typical individual, are sensitive to tone and pay acute attention to how something is shared with them. And, yes, some of them are even geniuses of the first order.

BAD NEWS

Don't hide bad news from your faculty and internal leaders. They will only gossip if you do. And as possible, share bad news in person, admitting what is difficult and what might be a silver lining.*

The admonition that bad news should be shared in person (while good news can be shared in any way) is perhaps too well-known to be worth repeating. But it is shared in case you are a new provost or dean and have not yet learned this lesson. Provosts and deans often find themselves in a position where they must share bad news. If you face such a need, remember that nothing communicates respect and investment in a faculty member more than you taking the time and trouble to share bad news in person. With as much honesty and generosity as possible, the act of speaking in the presence of the other, especially around difficult topics, communicates investment and respect. Similarly, sending a quick congratulatory email when there is good news likewise speaks of your investment in and care for your faculty, staff, students and alumnae. And don't forget the continuing power of a handwritten note. A short handwritten note of thanks or congratulations to an alumna or donor will do wonders for keeping your institution fresh and positive in their minds.

BEAUTY

Don't remain so entangled with busy work that you go a long stretch without bearing witness to beauty. Lewis Mumford's observation remains true: a day without sight or sound of beauty is a poverty-stricken day. And a succession of such days is fatal to human life.

In any given year, you, as an academic leader, will face a never-ending list of administrative and personnel challenges. Given that most of those challenges will be urgent, it will be entirely natural and easy for you to continually set aside such non-urgent endeavors as seeking out moments of wonder, whether that means spending time in nature or soaking in works of art (visual, musical, theatrical, etc.). If you don't take time to seek out moments of wonder, however, your reservoir will slowly but surely deplete. Put simply, your soul – that center that provides you with creativity and resilience – needs nourishment. And you need opportunities to do more than just calm your anxieties. While taking time to rest will slightly rejuvenate your body and mind, and while such acts as sharing words of thanks or congratulations will temporarily buoy your spirits, those acts will not go so deep as to truly refresh your soul. Lewis Mumford was hardly exaggerating in describing the effect of a succession of beauty-less days. William Wordsworth put it differently when he described the impact of being bogged down in busy-ness: "The world is too much with us; late and soon, / Getting and spending, we lay waste our powers." (See, also, "Exercise.")

BIG PICTURE

Don't get too caught up focusing on details. As a leader, you are paid in part to think strategically about the big picture. If you don't consider the big picture, no one else will.

The issue is not that you must always focus on the big picture. There are certainly times when you need to work with a team on tactics and details. But as an academic leader (especially when you are a provost or dean), you are uniquely positioned to have the opportunity and perspective to consider the big picture. What is your school's mission and vision? What are the most important two or three things that your school and community truly need to tackle or accomplish in the year ahead? What is your school succeeding at, and where are there true opportunities for improvement? What are the most important areas of your leadership work that you need to further strengthen? Questions like these belong squarely in your court, and you are not only responsible for asking them, but for bringing people together to have them answered in a way that aligns your leadership team in a shared sense of purpose.

BOTTOM LINE

Don't forget that the ultimate business of education is the business of educating, of supporting student learning and development. If you have a difference of opinion with faculty, consider the issue from the standpoint of student welfare and success.

With very few exceptions, higher education institutions have become complex business organizations with multiple areas of focus and concern. It is easy for an academic leader at times to be so caught up with competing stakeholders – faculty, staff, students, alumni, donors, trustees, regional communities, government officials, grant-funding entities, and parents of students – that decision-making becomes fraught with ambiguity and stressed by the pressure of competing interests. You will not be alone in occasionally forgetting that your core business is educating students. The best time to recall that fact is, of course, at the very moment things are most fraught. You will lose nothing and gain much – especially at moments when there is disagreement with or among faculty – by asking what is best for student welfare and success. That question will help ground your thinking and the thinking of others.

BUDGET MODELS

Don't lose sleep over the budget model employed at your college or university. Regardless of the one used, there will be glaring drawbacks. Budgeting in higher education is a high-stakes game. Learn the rules and play it as best you can.

There is much disagreement within higher education as to which budgeting model is best. Activity-based? Zero-based? Performance-based? Incremental? Responsibility Center Management? It is not uncommon for an institution to switch budgeting models, confident that the new model will provide further opportunity for financial stability and better align the institution with strategic priorities. Invariably, the new budget model will create as many problems as it will solve. Your job as an academic leader is to become an expert in the system of budgeting employed at your institution so that you can use it to best advantage for the growth and success of your school or program and people. Don't become too jealous of the model you hear about from a fellow leader at another institution. Rest assured that the budget model they have to deal with has its own significant disadvantages.

BUDGET OFFICERS

Don't forget to mentor those in your faculty and staff who are budget officers. Their success or failure in managing funds will be seen as yours.

Perhaps the word "mentor" above is a tad strong. The point is that your superiors necessarily hold you ultimately responsible for the condition of your budgets. One of the best ways you can mentor is by setting an example. Show your faculty and staff how you approach your own budget with a spirit that is not only reasonable and frugal but creative. In demonstrating your readiness to invest in innovative faculty and initiatives, for example, you better encourage your own budget officers to see their budgets not only as frameworks to support necessary purchases, but also as strategic assets.

CAREER ADVANCEMENT

Don't focus on professional success. Cherish moments with faculty and colleagues, prioritizing purpose over ambition and wealth.*

There are certainly senior academic leaders out there with CVs revealing an employment record that has them within one position or institution for only two or three years at a time. Consider, a three-year term means an academic leader will spend one year becoming familiar with a role and building relationships within a community, one year immersed in the role, and the last year engaged in job hunting. Individuals who are continually focused on rising up a ladder – whether advancing in the level of administrative position or reputation of institution – have limited life-enriching connections to their communities. By all means, if you find yourself in a position that is a poor fit, seek a different opportunity. But strive to be as generous with yourself as possible; open yourself up to moments of joy where you are, with people where you are.

CHANGE

Don't assume people always resist change. Understand that people are more likely to resist the way change is pursued. That said, change is difficult for us all. As James Baldwin observed, people can cry much easier than they can change.

It is vital that you, as a new or aspiring academic leader, understand the two interrelated points above: that how change is pursued is more important than what change is pursued; and regardless of how it is pursued, change is (with very few exceptions) difficult. If you keep those two realities in mind, you will spare yourself and your faculty much grief. There are few things more ill-fated than academic initiatives focused on significant change which don't include broad ownership or don't follow a process well communicated to all. If you need a checklist of how to pursue change, there are few better than that designed by Erika Andersen. Her research-based advice might be summarized as follows. First, increase understanding, continually reinforcing what the change is, why it's happening, and what the future will be post-change. Second, in addition to clarifying what isn't changing, reinforce what priorities/values are supporting and being supported by the envisioned change. Finally, give control and support to those helping to lead the change. All this said, know that even a diligent pursuit of all of the above won't guarantee the absence of nay-sayers. You will always have those who drag their heels and complain in the rear. The goal is to ensure they are very much in the minority.

CHOICES

Don't always look for a good solution. Sometimes your choice will be between a so-so solution and a truly horrid one. You will need to make some hard decisions at times, decisions that involve risk.

A not insignificant portion of the problems that reach senior academic leaders involve complex and intractable issues with hard-to-discern solutions. Put differently, a fair number of problems reaching you will have a bad, a worse, and a truly unacceptable solution. Your job will be to limit damage as much as possible. And remember, one of the reasons you are paid what you are is because the job you do is unpleasant at times. If you have built your capacity for sound judgment, have developed techniques to outsmart your own biases, and have learned to trust your gut, you will be better able to choose or create solutions that provide the greatest chance for the best possible outcome. Celebrate when you face a problem with easily discernable good and bad solutions; it may well be followed by a problem with no good solutions. (See, also, "Intuition.")

CIVILITY

Don't be blind to its shortcomings. At times, civility can obscure the marginalization of others and be a powerful ally of the status quo. Remember, incessant politeness is often less civility than it is cowardice in the face of needed change.

It wasn't that many years ago that educational leaders comfortably promoted civility as a paramount value. What has become increasingly apparent, however, is that civility – as an orientation and set of rules for communication – is especially valuable to those who would guard the status quo against challenge. Repeatedly, we have seen that civility – no loud protests, please! – can support the interest of those in power and be effective in ensuring the ongoing marginalization of the powerless. There is a time and place for loud protest. Of course, discerning that appropriate time and place is far from easy. Use as your measure two core priorities: ensuring the well-being of the most vulnerable; and safeguarding the integrity of intellectual and artistic work. (See, also, "Impartiality.")

COMPLAINTS

Don't lose track of your replies to angry external emails, letters, or phone messages. Those replies deserve not only your prudence but also your creativity and good humor. Craft them carefully, and keep them easily accessible for future reference.

One of the most challenging areas of communication facing academic leaders is that with a disgruntled or angry parent, donor, or member of the public. Your need to respond is an opportunity to further build your bank of prudent and creative responses; responses that both acknowledge the concerns being raised and affirm your school's or program's core values as related to those concerns. If the focus of the complaint relates to a faculty or staff member, be sure to explain that while you cannot discuss any particulars related to personnel issues, you will be following up on the shared concern. Of course, if there is any mention of lawyers in the complaint you receive, immediately forward the communication to your university counsel, and don't make any reply unless so advised by that counsel (using language approved by same).

CONTRADICTION

Don't constantly seek to eliminate contradiction, impatiently reaching after fact and reason. There can be more than one truthful account of an incident or circumstance.

Perhaps no metaphor can be more helpful to you when dealing with a faculty possessing hurt feelings or sporting offense than the following. Great discomfort can as easily come from a small and sharp pebble in a shoe as it can from a serious wound. If you face an aggrieved faculty or staff member, and find the offending action or situation to be minor, resist being dismissive. Even if you feel you know all the facts, there may be an additional and contradictory account that is also truthful. It is quite likely that around any incident, individuals will necessarily possess differing truths. The most useful path forward, you will often find, will be to approach faculty involved in an incident or unfortunate circumstance with an eye to finding out how each wishes to see the issue resolved. Just by listening and understanding, you will go a long way to make those faculty feel heard and to decrease the offense or pain.

CRITICAL THINKING

Don't chase definitions of this every time a curriculum committee considers it anew. Critical thinking is, ultimately, a highly contrived activity, and proficiency in it is achieved only with great effort, and often at great expense. Remember, too, it is domain specific. That someone thinks with exceptional clarity in one domain does not mean they won't make poor judgments and act a fool in another.

The above reflection touches on what seems to be the three most brazen and ongoing misperceptions of critical thinking. First, that it is a relatively natural undertaking and similarly accessible to all. Second, that it has no negative qualities, which is to say that its development is necessarily entirely without downsides. And third, that once gained it enables individuals to think critically across disciplines and domains. As research has now made abundantly clear, none of these three assertions have merit. Of course, the appropriate response is not to give up on the enterprise but to pursue it with the humility and circumspection it deserves.

CURRICULUM

Don't begin discussions around curriculum by focusing on courses or course sequence. Encourage faculty to always begin curriculum discussions with a focus on values and priorities. Curriculum, after all, is first and foremost a reflection of same.

As the social sciences repeatedly teach us, what is easiest to measure is rarely that which will give the most insight into an issue. Along similar lines, what is easiest to define in curriculum – credit hours, course descriptions and titles – is hardly that which is most important in a course of study. Strongly encourage your faculty to begin any course or program revision by asking what values, learning outcomes, or areas of skill they wish to see improved in students. And hold them honest to not take shortcuts in shaping an answer. It is only when they are certain of the bigger issue they wish to address or solve that they should feel free to talk about such details as credit hours and course titles and sequences.

CUSTODIAL STAFF

Don't ignore custodial staff. A kind word will do wonders for their sense of feeling welcomed and respected.

Make no mistake about it, the feel of a community is influenced by how those employees who earn the lowest salary levels are treated. Consider, if you are taking the time to be kind to your custodial staff, you are on your way to understanding and acting on the importance of treating all with respect and consideration. And if you set that example as a department chair, dean or provost, it is all the more likely that others will follow. The advice you receive during childhood remains important: treat all you meet with kindness.

DEANSHIP / PROVOSTSHIP

Don't assume that being a dean or provost is necessarily sustainable. There may be a point when you need to step away from that work. If you feel it's time, step down and away as you can.

Many deanships and provostships involve multi-year and renewable contracts. And it is easy to believe that if an institution or school is benefitting from your leadership and vision, then you have the responsibility to continue in your role. But consider, is your mental or physical health wearing thin? Has your drive and sense of hope diminished to a point where you no longer awake with an eager eye to the challenges and opportunities ahead? If you are commonly experiencing any of those things, consider stepping away from your role. Perhaps your financial commitments will make such an exit difficult for you or your family. If that's the case, weigh the true costs carefully. But remember, the potential cost of burnout is severe. It can debilitate to an extent that even the most extended of vacations will necessarily be inadequate to provide recovery.

DIFFICULT STRETCHES

Don't expect that because you were the enthusiastic choice of faculty, things will always be bright and breezy. Neither you nor your faculty are perfect, and you will need to be continually vigilant against stepping on each other's feet.

New chairs, deans and provosts might be surprised to learn that a not insignificant number of highly skilled academic leaders depart their roles somewhat bitter or even disillusioned, hurt when a seemingly strong working relationship with faculty was suddenly shaken through an unexpected change in circumstance or through the hostile or unpleasant behavior of one or more faculty. Be mindful that your success is never entirely your own doing, nor that of the faculty and community, nor that of the university leadership, nor that of the circumstance and fit. Your success, rather, is a slightly mysterious and ever-changing combination of all those things. Put differently, the dance between academic leaders and their faculty is never entirely secure. In fact, the more virtuosic the dance is, the greater the opportunity all have to step on each other's feet and stumble. (See, also, "Followers" and "Leadership.")

DIRECT REPORTS

If you are a provost or dean, don't interfere with the managerial responsibilities of your immediate reports. Few things upset internal leaders more than interference in matters of detail from their boss.*

If you have gained a senior position of leadership, it is in good part because you possess strengths in many skills and competencies employed by the faculty and academic leaders who report to you. It might be easy at times for you to engage with details in their work. Avoid that temptation. If you need to bring attention to some small aspect of a project or initiative they are leading, do so inviting their sense-making of the issue. Ultimately, there is nothing more important for leaders entrusted to do certain tasks than to feel they are indeed continually trusted with their responsibilities. If there is an egregious misstep in some managerial responsibility by one of your deans or associate/assistant deans, outline it directly and, when possible, provide them with a clear second opportunity to succeed. (Don't lose sight of the fact that to be human is to err and to be deserving of second chances.) Ensuring and respecting an opportunity to succeed also means respecting their opportunity to fail. Be fair in holding them accountable.

DISCUSSIONS

Don't stifle discussions in your faculty meetings. Let each faculty member contribute ideas.

With rare exceptions, disagreement within a community is a sign of vitality. General Patton was likely right when he asserted that when everyone agrees, someone is not thinking. Of course, decision-making should not be frozen by disagreement. An academic leader's objective, rather, should be to ensure that all voices are heard and that disagreement is approached with generosity. It is of great importance that a faculty member who sees something everyone else is missing should feel comfortable speaking up. An important clarification: the extent to which your faculty will have complementary and differing perspectives (and be able to contribute to creative solutions) is greatly dependent upon the extent to which they come from diverse backgrounds. As organizations of all types continually discover, a homogenous group of people has reduced capacity for truly creative thinking. (See, also, "Diversity" below.)

DIVERSITY

Don't relent in the work of strengthening your institution's commitment to diversity. Diversity is not a project to be completed as much as it is a value requiring ongoing support. A diverse community will be untidy and full of contradictions, but it will also have the greatest capacity to shape creative answers to seemingly intractable challenges.

This issue is as complex as it is important. Research has repeatedly shown multiple benefits when organizations and communities become more diverse (from fostering innovation and reducing stereotypes to further enabling people to live and prosper within diverse societies). But how can universities best make progress toward this end, especially in the typically under-expressed areas of racial, ethnic and gender diversity? Some studies suggest that instead of having a dedicated DEI administrative structure, institutions should focus on building shared equity leadership, dispensing more responsibilities and training across academic programs and student-focused offices. One popular tactic is ensuring senior university officials are disproportionally from underrepresented populations. However, many institutions have realized that achieving a symbolic milestone, like having a woman of color as university president, can create a false sense of progress. Regardless of the tactics you pursue, you will quickly find that it is impossible to do everything required to make speedy advance in this area. The point is to do the best possible with honesty, openness, generosity, and accountability. Of course, that openness has become harder given the ideological attacks that state legislatures have launched against DEI efforts and corresponding rulings from the supreme court. Yes, you will need to adopt numerous counteractive measures, beginning with relabeling initiatives. Also, be aware that your commitment to diversity may ultimately come into tension with your commitment to academic freedom. As multiple entities have noted (including the American Association of University Professors), it is sometimes exceedingly difficult to secure supportive space for a diverse group of students and for the vigorous exchange of ideas necessary for teaching and learning. There is no easy way forward. Our charge is as simple as its implementation is not: champion the vigorous exchange of ideas while also caring for the most vulnerable, including those from historically marginalized populations. (See, also, "Freedom, Academic," "Inclusion," and "Racism.")

DRUG USE

Don't be overly pious regarding drug use by those in your program or school. Approach with seriousness coupled with compassionate care. Drug use can as easily be the manifestation of someone caught in a vicious cycle as it can be the outcome of poor judgment.

Make no mistake, a no-exceptions, zero-tolerance policy around drug use by employees is a greater indicator of disregard for welfare than it is of courage to act on misdeeds. Yes, there are times when it is vital to act in a disciplinary way – a repeat offense, drug distribution, etc. And your institution's obligation to involve law enforcement will, of course, be determined by applicable laws. But always consider how you can approach the situation with an eye to care and generosity, both for your community and the individual involved. There are few things as precious in life (or as powerful an investment in a person's development) as providing second chances with care. Provide them also with clarity regarding expectations, and with support for meeting those expectations.

EDUCATION

Don't fret too much over theories of education, which remains one of the dullest subjects while also being one of the most complex of endeavors. If you cherish its central components – the passion of those who would imagine and mentor, and the hunger and courage of those who would learn and be changed – you will do well enough.

Enough said.

EMAILS

Don't ever send an email written in anger. And don't reply to emails or send texts in the late evening or on weekends. If you do, it will affirm that you are always available after hours.

Few minor issues have as great an impact on the well-being of individuals as email (and text) communication. The first of the above admonitions should be a no-brainer for any new academic leader. Much more is lost than gained when you send an email written in anger. The second admonition is a different matter. Many new academic leaders, energized by their new role, happily burn the midnight oil, engaging in any number of initiatives and issues after business hours and on weekends. Make no mistake, your leadership team and community are carefully observing the example you set. If you are not setting healthy personal boundaries when it comes to time, your leadership team and faculty will be less likely to as well. Many of us have learned the hard way that a neglected work/life balance takes a profound toll on our well-being. If there is an emergency, reach out by phone. Otherwise, don't send an email written in the evening or on a weekend, or use a time delay service to deliver it on the next business day. One final clarification: emails are a perfect example of a technology that has addressed some problems only to create powerful new ones. Though it might seem unusually cautious, consider setting specific times during workdays to check your email intentionally. Otherwise, you will experience email as the profound disrupter it can be. (The best analogy of that disruption? A

postal delivery person walking behind you and every couple of
minutes tapping you on the shoulder to pass you an envelope,
saying, "Here's another.")

EMPLOYMENT SECURITY — FOR PROVOSTS AND DEANS

Don't forget that, as a provost or dean, you typically work at the pleasure of the president or provost. That you had a brilliant year last year does not save you from potential criticism (including unfair criticism) in the current one.

What will give you the greatest possible security when the provost or president is considering restructuring, lay-offs, or changes to your employment status? Well, your track record of giving space and support for programmatic innovation and faculty achievement will surely be of help. And a good working relationship with faculty will also be of aid. Ultimately, however, what will be most helpful to your job security will be the presence of dynamic and positive relationships with donors and board of trustee members. No decision will be harder for a provost or president to make than one that is seen as questionable by important donors.

ENJOYMENT

Don't pass up opportunities to enjoy that which gives you true delight. Rabbi Rev was likely right: at judgment day, all will be judged according to what they might have enjoyed but did not.

Besides the presence of meaningful personal relationships, few things are as powerful an ally to your success in making it through hard times as your awareness of and access to those experiences and undertakings that give you true enjoyment. Yes, it is easier to pay attention to the welfare of others than to your own well-being. But doing so is not a sign of true generosity. Rather, it signals that you are failing to be as respectful of yourself as you are with others. Your capacity to support others when you aren't paying appropriate attention to yourself will always be short-lived. Without ongoing efforts to refill your reservoir of contentment and joy, your life as an administrator and leader will become overwhelmingly tedious and difficult. Strive to be as acutely aware of what gives you personal joy as you are diligent in the fulfillment of your work responsibilities.

ENTREPRENEURSHIP

Don't be afraid to use donor and discretionary monies to support the entrepreneurial work of faculty, staff, and students. There are more individuals around you with an entrepreneurial mindset than you realize. By all means, tie funding to clear parameters and goals, but then give your people space and support to create. Doing so will further vitalize your community and boost the spirit of those ready and eager to create.

As a leader with access to discretionary monies, you have repeated occasions to encourage and support the creativity and innovation of faculty, staff and students. If you constantly reward same, and frequently and publicly acknowledge it as an important part of how things are done at your school, you will better establish it as a norm in your community. And make no mistake, there is no area of higher education that is not in great need of an entrepreneurial approach by all involved. That includes everything from recruitment of students to curricula, from resource development to your community's commitment to inclusive excellence.

EXECUTIVE ASSISTANT

Don't assume there is anyone more important to your success. Give them the freedom and authority not only to manage your schedule but also to interrupt your schedule and even send you home when they observe you are not in shape to make sound decisions.

If you have an assistant, count yourself most fortunate. Yes, your assistant's ability to manage projects, communicate with multiple constituencies, and support your calendar and initiatives is vital. Even more important, however, is something that might initially seem too personal: your assistant's ability to help you monitor and manage your personal well-being. As you'll quickly discover, few things impact your ability to be engaged with issues at a high level as much as your general well-being. And, in a cruel twist, if you care deeply about the success of your school and community, it will often be easy for you to overlook your own well-being. That is where your assistant can strategically help you. Give your assistant permission to not only monitor your engagement and functioning, but to directly confront you if it's clear that you desperately need a brief break for some recovery or down time. Of course, once you give such permission, you must treat the advice received with respect.

EXERCISE

Don't give up whatever physical activity or outdoor sport you have been accustomed to just because you have become an academic leader with significant administrative responsibilities. There is wisdom to friluftsliv, the Norwegian concept and tradition of making time for the outdoors, regardless of the season. At the very least, physical activity will keep your mind and body from weakening too quickly.*

As a higher education leader, you are necessarily in a taxing position mentally and emotionally, and, thus, physically. Yes, some leaders might have the gift of unusual physical resilience and vitality. But in their leadership role, most will find that those things which take energy continually outpace those things which give energy. Which is to say, most will find that academic leadership is, overall, a net-negative undertaking. Your investment in exercise is a way to tip the scales back in the direction of your long-term well-being. Yes, the prospect of making an investment in exercise can be as tortuous for some as it is joyous for others. Choose carefully which type of exercise you pursue. Select with an eye to ensuring it is easily accessible to you and that it will give you some near-term joy. And yes, as research affirms, physical activity in the natural outdoors seems to yield especially positive rewards. (See, also, "Beauty" and "Solitude.")

FACULTY

Don't be quick to offer advice to faculty, and avoid arguing with a stubborn faculty member. Drop the matter before argument leads to temper. You can generally gain your point in some other way.

You likely have among your faculty individuals who are brilliant in their fields. A not insignificant portion of them will live under the assumption that their brilliance is pervasive, extending across multiple areas of life and work. There will be times when you will have no alternative but to approach a faculty member who not only possesses this attribute but also happens to be stubborn. Although there is no pathway that guarantees success when working with such a colleague, you will typically be rewarded if you approach them with an invitation to join you in problem solving. This is to say, if you must approach a stubborn and vain faculty member about an issue, be as clear regarding the issue and the reason why it must be addressed as possible. Then invite that colleague to help you understand the best path to get to that resolution. Yes, there's a chance they won't play along. But there's a still bigger chance that they will drop their guard at least a little and engage.

FACULTY SENATE

Don't miss opportunities to champion the faculty senate when you can. The ongoing corporatization of universities leaves many faculty feeling marginalized. The faculty senate is one of the too rare spaces where they can exert power and influence.

Faculty senate bodies differ significantly between institutions. Indeed, the relationship between a faculty senate and their institution's leadership team can range from collaborative to intractably adversarial. While a variety of factors determine the exact nature of the relationship, some factors play an especially influential role, such as the degree of trust and transparency between both entities and the institutional leadership team's comfort with making slower and more collaborative decisions. Virtually every time an institution further professionalizes an aspect of its operation or succumbs to pressure to make quick decisions on complicated financial and operational matters, it nudges towards operating more as a corporate entity rather than a deliberative body invested in shared governance. The net sum of those frequent nudges is a faculty increasingly out of the decision-making loop. It should not be surprising that the modern faculty senate is, with rare exceptions, much more committed to shared governance and democratic decision-making than an institution's president and leadership team. If that weren't enough, faculty senate bodies are usually poorly resourced, have little office support for their complicated work, are overseen by faculty receiving insufficient release

time, and typically pursue a roster of issues greater than available time would allow. Yet they remain the primary voice of
faculty on matters large and small. Support them as you can.
(See, also, "Freedom, Academic.")

FELLOW ACADEMIC LEADERS

Don't ignore any opportunity to learn from experienced fellow leaders. Even if their disciplinary field is different, they will have gained powerful insights.

Most of us have yet to meet an academic leader who hasn't learned some important lesson regarding leadership and working with faculty. If you happen to find yourself in conversation with fellow leaders, don't pass up the opportunity to learn what they've found difficult or easy, and what they've learned along the way that they wished they'd known at the start of their leadership work. It's very likely that you will learn something valuable in their response.

FOLLOWERS

Don't forget that followership can be fickle, and when the people who follow are faculty, even the goodwill that is earned through hard work can evaporate suddenly.

Perhaps there is no more important lesson to be learned about leadership than that it depends especially on the priorities and whims of followers. Faculty possess highly developed skills in their discipline (including the capacity to think critically regarding aspects of their domain). But they also have the human tendency to follow gut feelings when it comes to most things outside their disciplinary area of expertise, including administrators and bureaucratic processes. This is to say, their perception of you and your work can change swiftly and for reasons that have little to do with you. Be as steady a rock as you can, and don't take it too personally when faculty members suddenly think less of you. They may come around. Or not. (See, also, "Difficult Stretches" and "Leadership.")

FREEDOM, ACADEMIC

Don't let it diminish further. There are many implications to the ever-growing costs surrounding an institution's business functions and non-instructional student services. Some of those implications are obvious: less money for full-time faculty and a greater reliance on part-time faculty. Others are equally pernicious but obscured: communities becoming increasingly indifferent to academic freedom. Support it. Always.

All higher education institutions claim to support and value academic freedom. But with few exceptions, most continue to erode its presence as they further limit its two primary supports: shared governance and tenured full-time faculty. If faculty at your institution feel interference or pressure regarding the shape of curricula or the content and use of student evaluations, then your institution is hardly the bastion of academic freedom it purports to be. And if your institution is a public institution, you may well be living through ideological assaults on academic freedom as a result of state legislative action. If higher education is to champion critical inquiry and the free exchange of thoughtful ideas, it not only requires academic freedom for faculty but those foundational systems that support same. To the extent that your institution is increasingly relying on part-time faculty and making speedy and major decisions impacting academics without faculty input, then it is weakening its capacity to support and advance academic freedom. And, as explained above (see "Diversity"), be aware that your commitment to academic freedom may come into tension with your school's commitment to diversity (and inclusion). As multiple entities have noted, it is sometimes exceedingly difficult to secure supportive space for both a diverse group of students and also for the vigorous exchange of ideas necessary for learning. A subcommittee of the American Association of University Professors was perhaps oversimplifying that point in one report when it asserted the following: "Ideas that are germane to a subject under discussion in a classroom cannot be censored because a student with particular religious or political beliefs might be offended. ...This would create a classroom environment inimical to the free and vigorous exchange of ideas necessary for teaching and learning in higher education." There is, of course, no easy way forward. Our most fundamental charge is as simple as its implementation is not: champion the vigorous exchange of ideas while also caring for all, including the most vulnerable and those from historically marginalized populations.

FRIENDLINESS

Don't avoid being friendly to all. Even though your job, ultimately, is about elevating others and doing so equitably, you can be friendly. Friendship, you'll recall, is the thing that gives value to survival.

As has been stated in various ways over the centuries, happiness arises from friendship, and harmonious friendship is one of the few things which ease the burdens of life. A friend, as Seneca reflected, is someone you can speak with as boldly as you speak with yourself. Given the differences in power and authority, it will not be easy for you to build truly meaningful friendships with your own faculty and staff. That doesn't mean you shouldn't make an effort to be friendly. To have friendships of the type that truly nurture, you'll typically need to look outside your immediate school community. Invest in those meaningful friendships. They will help sustain you.

FRONT OFFICE STAFF

Don't be frugal regarding small items for your front office staff if your operational budget can afford to support them generously.

It remains true: who you are as an organization is significantly revealed by how the most vulnerable in your midst are treated. Make no mistake about it, your front office staff may be among the lowest paid of your salaried employees, but their impact is outsized, both on your community and its culture. Treat them as generously as you can. Few things will go as far in helping them feel valued as providing them with access to discretionary spending on things that will support or strengthen their professional success. They know, better than you, what they need that would further support success in their jobs. Give them an opportunity as you can to make that investment. (See, also, "Custodial Staff.")

FUNDRAISING

Don't so much seek to raise money as seek to connect people with projects that matter to them. The work of fundraising is not so difficult when its focus is building relationships and connecting people with ways of making a difference that excite them.

Increasingly, academic leaders are charged with engaging in fundraising. For many, this is an unwelcome reality. And to be clear, there are few experiences more miserable than asking for money from a person you don't really know for something you aren't passionate about. But conversely, the work of connecting people you know and have a relationship with to a cause or project that excites them and greatly benefits your community is an act that is as organic as it can be rewarding. Again, all three of those factors are vital: (1) you know and have a relationship with the person; (2) the receipt of the requested gift will make a marked and positive impact on some important aspect of your community (and is something you're excited about); and (3) the project in question is in an area of significant interest to the potential funder. To be sure, even with all three of those factors in place, the act of asking might still be a prickly affair. Many people, after all, have a complicated relationship with money. But if you ensure all three of the above factors are in place, you are creating the best possible circumstance for an ask that you (and your potential donor) can feel good about.

GENEROSITY

Don't expect to be thanked for your generous actions. Faculty assume you will act generously.*

If you are a newly installed academic leader, it's important that you understand the above advice. That your act of generosity requires much of you is of minor concern to most faculty. They are comfortable believing that an academic leader is necessarily a selfless leader. Considerable generosity is simply assumed.

GENIUS

Don't forget that one of the few things as important as genius is character. If you have some competence and your faculty find you honest and trustworthy, don't worry too much about the rest.

Anyone who has accepted and been granted a senior academic leadership role likely has a broader perspective and a more accommodating orientation than normal. Yes, you need to possess considerable intellect and success in your disciplinary field to earn the respect of faculty. As importantly, you need to be effective in playing the role (when needed) of coach, cheerleader, mentor, and guardian. Those roles are, of course, open to you to the extent you possess laudable character and emotional resilience. If you possess both, you don't need to be a genius. However, you do need to be quite smart.

GESTURES

Don't omit making small gestures of thanks and congratulations. Your faculty and staff may value even the smallest of handwritten notes for your thought of them.

There are few things easier to overlook than taking the time to write and send a note of thanks or congratulations. Make no mistake, those small gestures greatly aid your ability to maintain good working relationships. Your note doesn't have to be long; it simply needs to be honest and to the point. It means much to faculty that you are noticing their successes, and that you find them important and special as individuals. Yes, there will always be those who will remain unaffected by your kind gesture. (See "Generosity" above.) But more likely than not, your word will add a small and further ray of sunshine to the recipient's day. Never pass up an opportunity to craft and send a note of thanks or congratulations to your faculty and staff. Once it's a habit, it will be the easiest thing in the world. (See, also, "Ordinary Things.")

GOSSIP

Don't indulge in gossip during one-on-one meetings with faculty. That faculty member is like all, deserving of courtesy and the assurance that you do not betray confidences. And besides, it's poor form to meddle in the stuff of other people's souls.*

As provost, dean, or department chair, you will have insights into many confidential situations, and have unusual access to personal information about your faculty and staff. Indeed, the possession of that information and those insights contribute to the power of the position you inhabit. To confirm, it is easy (and quite natural) to be enticed by power and to make a public show of it. But your ability to keep this element of your position constantly hidden is of greatest importance. If you find yourself starting to gossip, make any excuse necessary to exit the conversation. No one will ever look poorly on your tendency to turn conversations away from gossip. Indeed, you will be respected all the more for not betraying confidence. And, yes, it is poor form to meddle in the stuff of other people's souls.

HAPPINESS

Don't chase it. If happiness has not found you, follow John Dewey's advice: find what you are truly fitted to do and secure an opportunity to do it. Happiness may follow.

Not much more needs to be said. Certainly, if you're seriously depressed or anxious, act on the understanding that therapy, medication and personal practice can help. Ultimately, the pursuit of happiness is as beguiling an act as it is pointless. (Helen Fisher was hardly exaggerating when she explained that we were not built to be happy but to reproduce.) Do good as you can, and work to make a positive difference both to yourself and those around you. The rest will likely fall into place.

HELPING DURING CRISIS

Don't be afraid to lend a hand in the dirtiest of work if there is a temporary and pressing crisis. It will do you no harm to sweep a flooded bathroom or comfort a stranger. Your staff have to do plenty of things they are unaccustomed to.

The notion of leading by example is never more pertinent than during moments of crisis. Your presence and participation are needed in those moments not because you will make all the difference but because it will communicate to your community that during difficult stretches, we all pitch in.

HOPELESS ENDEAVORS

Don't think that just because certain endeavors seem hopeless that there is no virtue in pursuing them. Sometimes the most meaningful pursuits are those seeking to address a cause or concern which seems largely or even entirely hopeless.

During your tenure as dean, you will often hear faculty speak of potential projects or initiatives that you strongly suspect are destined for failure. To the fullest extent possible, lean into those cherished proposed projects, and lend them your support. Nothing means more to faculty than receiving support for something close to their heart. (And your lack of generosity, if you withhold support from the beginning, will not easily be forgotten.) The opportunity to fail is an important one; we typically learn more from failure than we do from success. And besides, the opportunity for true success requires many opportunities for failure.

HUMOR

Don't forget to cultivate a sense of humor. It, too, is a source of wisdom, and will carry you safely past many a danger-signal at meetings.

It doesn't take much living to discover that humor is one of the most powerful tools to navigate through moments of difficulty. If you find yourself at an impasse during a meeting with faculty, share something humorous and self-deprecating. As you'll quickly discover, moments of wit and humor can relieve tensions unlike anything else. Humor is useful in even the smallest of difficult situations. Have you forgotten someone's name? Share with a sigh and a smile that you have had a completely scatterbrained day, and ask for their name and their forgiveness. You will never be resented for having introduced a moment of levity into moments of difficulty. Humor is indeed a source of wisdom. As Samuel Johnson suggested, the size of a person's understanding can be justly measured by their mirth. (See, also, "Solemnity.")

IMAGINATION

Don't assume that facts are the center of truth. Imagination has a truth that facts can only envy, and when combined with passion can inspire a community to undertake the impossible.

Perhaps there is no more important role for an academic leader than to capture and share stories or metaphors that spark imagination and speak to a community's values and aspirations. Why are such stories and metaphors important? Firstly, they can elicit powerful emotions, the very thing that best spurs us all to action. Secondly, they help to reinforce and strengthen concepts that listeners likely already share and value. And finally, they entice, attracting listeners' attention to a degree otherwise impossible. (As research has shown, the mind retains stories much better than statistics.) If you're not a natural and imaginative storyteller, work on that skill. In the end, it's a straightforward thing. What is required is that you pay special attention to the many stories happening in your midst – whether related to students, alumni, faculty, or donors. Among those stories will be some that tug at you for reasons you may or may not be able to explain. Hold on to and consider those with care. And be ready to share them at what strikes you as the right moment. Practice this, and your skillfulness – your ability to go with your gut – will grow. (See, also, "Knowledge" and "Logic.")

IMPARTIALITY

Don't overlook the limits of impartiality. In certain circumstances, its maintenance supports the continuation of injustice.

If you are prone to believing that rational thought is of greater value than emotions, you might also assume (falsely) that your job is to be objective and impartial. The fact is that your job, including during moments of conflict, is not so much to be objective but to be kind. Is there someone within the situation who is especially vulnerable? Your obligation to their safety and security is paramount. Is there someone within the situation who has been unfairly treated in the past? Your obligation, again, is especially to ensure they are treated with renewed kindness. Always keep in mind that it is rare that our individual circumstances might be fully known by others. If your default orientation is to kindness, you will rarely go astray. (See, also, "Civility.")

INCLUSION

Don't forget that inclusion isn't an act as much as it is a continually affirmed commitment. Even a temporary slip-up in its application can marginalize individuals who feel themselves on the fringes.

The creation and maintenance of an inclusive community is impossible without ongoing action and affirmation. Yes, it is entirely natural for you and your leadership team to take pains to help a new faculty or staff member who might feel marginalized or come from an underrepresented population to feel welcome and included when they join your community. However, it is just as easy, and natural, to move on and fail to undertake further action that would ensure they continue to feel included. The need for ongoing action and support is easily discerned by you asking a simple question: is that individual forging strong social connections with others within their immediate and larger community? Do you see them easily laughing in a conversation with colleagues? If the answer to either is no, take extra effort to see that they are included in moments large and small, and have further opportunity to build relationships that might matter to them.

INCOMPETENCE

Don't hire even slightly incompetent people, regardless of their self-assurance. Charles Darwin's observation remains true: ignorance more frequently begets confidence than does knowledge. People who are incompetent do not and cannot recognize just how incompetent they are.

It is natural for us to be attracted to gregarious and enthusiastic individuals. It is equally natural for us to assume that individuals possessing those qualities are highly skilled in their work. Those two qualities, however, are unrelated. When considering individuals to hire into your community, give as great attention to the soft-spoken faculty or staff candidate (who might be exceptionally gifted in their work) as you approach with caution the outspoken candidate. The difference in impact between a highly competent individual and a mildly competent individual is outsized. If your candidate has an area of weakness, make sure it is of a type they can easily address and possess a desire to address. (See, also, "Introverts.")

INTELLECTUALS

Don't lose track of the true intellectuals in your community, those individuals who, as Julien Benda explained, are extraordinarily gifted and moral, bearing the conscience of all. Seek their advice often.

Each faculty community will have at least one or more of those true intellectuals, as described above. Make it a habit to check in with them often. Have a draft of a speech you will be giving to a larger group of your faculty and students? Run it by them to get feedback. They will have further insight into what is right for the moment. Having difficulty making sense of a complicated situation? Share it with them without betraying confidences, and ask for their thoughts. They will possess a further understanding of what to look out for and be able to see that situation with additional perspective.

INTROVERTS

Don't fail to give the additional time your introverted faculty need to contribute to discussions. Though often the most reluctant to engage, they can possess the greatest insights.

Academic leaders discover quite quickly that those faculty and staff who say the least sometimes have richer insights than those who talk most freely. No, don't discount what your talkative faculty and staff say. Just ensure there is good and continued opportunity for those who haven't spoken to speak. (See, also, "Discussions.")

INTUITION

Don't look at facts first when it comes to a major decision. At the start, check your intuition. Then practice due diligence. If you have learned to trust your gut and to outsmart your biases, you will likely make the right decision.

Successful leadership is, above all, the presence of an alignment between the leader's values and skills and the aspirations and values of those who would follow. If you were entirely honest and open at your job interview, understand that you were chosen in good part because of a sense of alignment. The way to ensure ongoing alignment is to first and foremost pay attention to your gut. No, you shouldn't blindly follow it; leaders can easily make mental errors based on hidden biases. Indeed, when facing a particularly large or complex decision, it will always be prudent to ensure your own biases aren't dictating your thinking. If you are surrounded by others who are leaning in a direction that you continue to find problematic at a gut level, speak to the factors which might be causing you discomfort. Even more importantly, ask for help to better understand what you might be missing. Occasionally, your gut might be reacting to incomplete information or one of your own hidden biases.

ISOLATION

Don't forget to stay in touch with your personal friends. Becoming an academic leader (and, especially, a senior academic leader) necessarily means becoming further isolated in your work environment. Having friends will keep you honest and will nourish your soul.

For virtually all of us, stepping into a leadership position means assuming a role that is quite isolated and isolating. Quite typically, our peers are exceptionally busy. And, not infrequently, we have little in common with our immediate superiors. If we are deans or provosts, our school communities are full of people who, one way or another, report to us. The absence of an ability to form friendships in our community is problematic. After all, nothing helps us remain grounded as much as honest feedback from friends. It is in friendship that difficult ideas are considered with care. It is in friendship that we find ways to ease the burdens of life. Keep in touch with your personal friends as you can. You never know when something you say, or they say, will make all the difference in the world. (See, also, "Friendliness.")

JUDICIOUSNESS

Don't imagine you can (or should) solve all significant challenges. As farmers know, it is often better to plow around a stump.

Not all battles are worth fighting. To be judicious as a department chair, dean, or provost means not only understanding how to navigate challenges, but discerning between those which deserve confrontation and those which are best left untouched. There will be few things more central to your ultimate success than your track record of having identified and prioritized the right challenges to confront. Each year, you will make one or two decisions that truly matter, decisions that will greatly impact your community. Keep an eye out for those decision points, understanding which challenges and opportunities truly matter. (See, also, "Problem Solving.")

KINDNESS

Don't simply be kind when needed. Do as James Barrie suggested: always try to be a little kinder than necessary.

There are many practical reasons why an orientation of kindness matters to academic leaders, and to all others in positions of power. Perhaps none is more powerful than the reason shared by Maya Angelou: "I've learned that people will forget what you said, people will forget what you did, but people will never forget how you made them feel."

KNOWLEDGE

Don't assume that a sound argument will enable understanding. Minds are difficult things to open, and the best way to open them, as we repeatedly find, is through the heart. Through, that is to say, stories that resonate.

To state what should be obvious, we are not thinking machines that feel but feeling animals that think. Need to bolster an argument? By all means, bring along some data. But even more importantly, bring along a powerful story or two. As we're often reminded, we are much more easily convinced by stories than data. (See, also, "Imagination" and "Logic.")

LARGE CHALLENGES

Don't continually keep your faculty leaders unaware of your large challenges. You will often find that their fresh minds will see a way out of some difficulty that has not occurred to you.

As most academic leaders quickly discover, having access to a variety of perspectives can greatly increase the clarity of a challenge, together with its possible solutions. Don't hesitate to engage your faculty leaders around large-scale problems. You will lose little and likely gain much by approaching them and engaging them by stating, "I have a sense of a good way forward, but I'd be interested to hear your perspectives on this." It's not difficult to both honor your responsibility to make tough decisions and to respect the wisdom of others. (See, also, "Judiciousness.")

LARGE PROJECTS

Don't assume that big things can be advanced based simply on their merit. Often, that advancement is supported only when trust has been built between you and faculty. Building that trust takes time, time which includes much honest discussion and transparent decision-making.

Even with the rosiest of beginnings, an academic leader will typically have to wait a while to gain the trust needed to truly confront large and complex challenges. As stated above, it is often only when faculty have witnessed repeated examples of honesty and transparency on your part that they will be ready to join you in truly tackling large and difficult projects. Of course, if the leader previous to you did not have a trusting relationship with faculty, the building of same will require even more time and work. If that is your situation, be patient with your faculty and with yourself. (See, also, "Respect.")

LEADERSHIP

Don't just provide leadership; build leaders. And don't think leadership is primarily about you and what you do. It is context specific, about what opportunities you can recognize and what followers are able to do related to those opportunities given their values and your support and example.

What, ultimately, is most vital for you as an academic leader to know and understand about leadership practice? Likely just three things. That it is important you work to strengthen the presence of internal leaders. That you spend time identifying important opportunities for organizational development, and increase the ability of faculty and staff to pursue major and innovative projects of value to them and your school. And, finally, that you should act not only understanding your own strengths and weaknesses but also with an eye to care and compassion. If you do that, you will build trust and do much of what any good academic leader can hope to do. (See, also, "Difficult Stretches" and "Followers.")

LEADERSHIP TEAM

Don't show your worst side to the leaders reporting to you. You need to be well thought of by your leadership team even more than by others. Let them have the benefit of your best qualities.

There are probably few temptations that are greater for a provost or dean than to collapse in a chair and complain to one or more of your senior leaders about this or that. But as the above advice states, there are pressing and important reasons why you should not succumb to that temptation. If you need to vent, do so to a fellow dean or provost with whom you have a close relationship or to a close personal friend outside of your scholarly community. You will never regret having acted courteously and professionally in front of your senior leadership team. And make no mistake, your senior leaders are learning from you how to act with their immediate reports. (See, also, "Gossip.")

LEARNING

Don't pass up any opportunity to increase your full-time faculty. As has repeatedly been shown, learning happens in relationships, and the relationship between a student and teacher typically grows best when the teacher is a full-time employee.

If immediate cost is the only factor, you will never win the argument for a full-time faculty member over an adjunct. But you can occasionally win that argument if your institution is especially interested in student learning and experience. With few exceptions, full-time faculty and staff (as compared with part-timers) have a greater capacity to engage in hallway conversations, build long-term relationships with students and colleagues, and manage and overhaul curricula based on lessons learned. Of course, any school can have those full-time faculty who are disengaged from student learning, and indifferent (at best) to interacting with students. If you happen to have several such faculty in your community, I extend my sympathies. All of the above is not to say that part-time faculty and staff are not essential. After all, they can bring fresh industry perspectives, can plug what would otherwise be holes in your curricular offerings, and can further connect students with relevant employing organizations. But the general point remains, don't pursue part-time faculty and staff at the expense of your full-timers. At every chance, support and strengthen the pool that is your full-time employees. (And, of course, invest in those who are energized by the opportunity to build relationships with learners.) By investing in such full-time employees, you will be investing not only in the quality of relationships between faculty/staff and students, but also in the quality of learning and research across your school.

LEGALITIES

73

Don't be primarily legal-minded. Be fair-minded first, legal-minded second.

It's simple, really. In the face of a particularly thorny issue, first ask what is the fair thing to do, then ensure you know what legal action is legal. You cannot do something which is illegal. But, for the integrity and vitality of your community, you must not do something which is unfair. That an action is legal doesn't mean it is also advisable.

LIBERAL ARTS EDUCATION

Don't dismiss its potential and the inspiration its ideal form can provide, even as you remain mindful of its limitations as an agent for human transformation and its legacy of further enriching the fortunate.

With the world around us simultaneously fixated on technological progress, the acquisition of material goods, increased natural disasters, growing animosity between political groups, and the like, there is flagging interest in listening to those proclaiming the virtues and benefits of liberal arts education. It does not matter that we have evidence that a type of liberal arts education can sometimes help produce captains of industry and successful social leaders and can spur the training of the mind. The water is too muddied. Arguments about it are typically tedious, and its exact parameters and content remain under contention. Such qualities as openness to surprise, aversion to forced conclusions, and tolerance of paradox and ambiguity are less likely the outcomes of its pursuit as they are achieved manifestations of innate qualities and predilections and/or aftereffects of fortunate circumstances. Most damningly, we have evidence that a good number of its core qualities have shortcomings as agents of positive change. As George Steiner rightly noted regarding Nazism, the ultimate political barbarism prevailed on the very ground of Christian humanism, Renaissance culture and classic rationalism. The ideal of liberal arts training is, of course, more than those things. So, can it enrich the soul? Seneca posited that the liberal arts (broadly imagined) don't bestow virtue as much as prepare the soul for same. Of course, implementation of a liberal arts education is always imperfect, and its ideal is rarely, if ever, attained. Put simply, as a model and product, it ultimately offers more promise than it guarantees benefits. Treat it with the respect and mild suspicion it deserves.

LIFE INSURANCE

Don't neglect life insurance, particularly as a senior academic leader. Overseeing people is taxing work, and a generous life insurance policy will protect your loved ones should you die suddenly.*

There are few things that stress a mind and body more than frequently dealing with complex personnel issues. And if you are a provost or dean, your days will be quite full of such dealings. In accepting that reality, you face a choice regarding how generous you will be with your loved ones and their welfare. Don't skimp on your life insurance. There are few worthier investments.

LISTENING

Don't ever forget to listen. Listen more than you talk, and you will be less likely to make regrettable decisions.

There is almost always something to be learned from others. And giving others the opportunity to speak will further reassure them that they are being heard. If there is a hole in an argument, your search for understanding will best enable the truth to emerge, as made sense by you both. Your decisions will only be as good as the information you have and the wisdom of your intuition. The easiest way to make a regrettable decision is to make it quickly, without truly listening to the insights of others.

LIVING SITUATION

Don't be extravagant in your spending, even if your current salary permits it. Few will resent you if you appear prudent, pursuing elegance rather than luxury.*

Faculty certainly understand that you earn more for doing work that most of them would never wish to do. And they will certainly feel comfortable seeing that you have good taste, whether in your appearance or your dwelling and possessions. But there is a difference between displaying good taste and offering a garish display of wealth. Faculty will be content with the former and resentful of the latter.

LOGIC

Don't fret that there may be little logic to some faculty behavior. We are not thinking machines that feel, we are feeling animals that think. All of us remain full of proclivities and vulnerabilities, with fancies which may be pleased.

The point here is not that faculty are unique as described above. Rather, and as researchers frequently explain, humans in general operate more on feelings than rational thought. Most people, as we've repeatedly found, reject the primacy of evidence and data. For most, the road to persuasion or action is through something that stirs the soul, such as a resonant story. We are more sentimental than rational, and yes, we are also driven by deeply seated fancies and proclivities. The sociobiologist E.O. Wilson put it differently, explaining that the real problem of humanity is that we have Paleolithic emotions, medieval institutions and godlike technology. (See, also, "Imagination" and "Knowledge.")

LYING

Don't lie to your faculty about anything. If they catch you lying, they might not trust you again.*

A high level of trust, as you no doubt have found, takes much time to establish and little time to lose. There will be many times when, whether to guard a confidence or put a positive spin on bad news, you will be tempted to stretch the truth in front of faculty. To the fullest extent possible, avoid that temptation. What you will gain is nothing compared to what you will lose.

MAGNETISM

Don't stay too close in orbit to magnetic and boisterous personalities. There is genius in the vivacious spirit, but an awkward truth remains: magnetism and dynamism often lean toward chaos.

We've all known them: the larger-than-life personalities that draw people in. If your faculty is a sizable group, you will likely have at least a few individuals like that in your community. Whether they are full of exceptionally creative (and difficult to implement) ideas or individuals who rely on charm to be persuasive, be supportive but keep your guard up. Yes, great ideas and significant breakthroughs have sometimes been achieved because of the presence of magnetism. But, as many have occasionally found, exceptional levels of magnetism and dynamism can precede moments of chaos.

MANAGEMENT SKILLS

Don't dwell on any lack of managerial perfection in your program directors if you are a dean. Support them as you can, understanding that integrity of spirit is more important than brilliance in management.

Count yourself lucky if you, as dean, have program chairs or directors with strong management skills. Yes, do give your academic leaders opportunities to take seminars or workshops to develop skills related to academic administration. But accept, too, that some will necessarily remain awkward as operational managers. Support them as you can. Express thanks for their leadership achievements when they have them. And understand that the most egregious actions relate not to underdeveloped management skills but to affairs of the soul, to misbehavior and deceit.

MANIPULATION

Don't manipulate others. Others will likely do that to you if you try to manipulate them.

You have power and authority within your leadership position. (Doubly so if you are a provost or dean.) With that power comes opportunity to manipulate others in ways large or small. It will be easy for you – especially in moments of crisis – to engage in generalization, withhold critical information, or play on a faculty or staff member's insecurities. Your engagement in such activities will necessarily undermine your working relationships and lead others to engage in similar behavior with you.

MISCHIEF MAKERS

Don't overlook the value of having (and ensuring support for) mischief makers in your midst. There are few individuals of greater value than those who push against norms and traditions without overly offending others.

The worth of mischief makers is typically undervalued. Yet the best mischief makers are exactly the type of individuals who spur innovation and help communities achieve complex goals. Their capacity to do so relates to their unique combination of traits. They typically have a fairly keen understanding of lines that shouldn't be crossed. They often have a sense of humor that reduces tension in tricky situations and supports progress in action. They typically possess not only impatience and resilience but also an ability to connect to others, traits that help them effectively pursue and attain tricky and long-term goals. All that said, there are some caveats. Roles do matter. The traits of a good mischief maker might be of greater value in a teaching faculty member than in an Associate Dean for Administration. Mischief makers, as described above, can be easily alienated, whether because they don't feel a sense of belonging or they falter from a lack of self-care. They are often outwardly facing, easily neglecting their own well-being. Keep a caring eye on their welfare.

MONEY

Don't expect happiness if you take a more senior administrative role for money.[*]

Few things are as ineffective as salary levels in providing individuals with a continued sense of purpose and resiliency in the face of difficulty. Yes, having a larger salary goes a long way to tweaking your living situation and supporting the welfare of your loved ones. But if you don't have a passion for the challenging responsibilities that come with your leadership role, no salary level will keep you engaged and resilient. Being an academic leader is, with few exceptions, far too stressful a position for anyone whose primary objective is the pursuit of a larger salary. (See, also, "Deanship / Provostship.")

NEW PROJECTS

Don't constantly increase the work of faculty by repeatedly adding tasks related to your new projects or ideas.

There is a good chance that you achieved your leadership role because you are unusually creative and full of innovative ideas. Few things will be easier for you than advocating for and allocating resources to an additional initiative you believe is important. Your motives might be laudable. For example, you might have suddenly envisioned an additional initiative that would further support your community's progress around diversity, equity, and inclusion. Understand, however, that faculty differ greatly in their ability to bear heavy loads and focus on multiple projects. Respect that, and spend the time needed to understand which initiatives should truly be prioritized. Most of us will do a few things very well, or many things poorly.

ONLINE LEARNING

Don't assume it is either the answer to all your school's ills or a fad that you should approach with caution. At its best, online learning can support high-quality learning and teaching while increasing access for students and decreasing net instructional costs.

At its best... Those three words are of central importance in the above statement. The following fact cannot be overstated: for your online degrees to support high-quality learning, they will require substantial and specialized resources, and their delivery and maintenance will require expertise not found in most traditional academic communities. As many academic leaders have found, it is more prudent and effective to create a separate space where online specialists can partner with faculty to deliver high-quality online teaching in special degrees than to try to nudge current in-person instruction and degrees towards hybrid or fully online delivery. Unfortunately, many institutions are unable or unwilling to invest the resources needed to ensure high-quality experiences for online learners.

ORGANIZATIONAL CULTURE

Don't forget to give organizational culture its due. Love your institution for what it is and what it can become. And remember that what is good policy at one institution may not be good at another.

If you remember to always love your school for what it is and what it can become, it will be easier for the fit between you and your school to be maintained, and it will be harder for you to make missteps around the culture of your school community. Perceiving your school this way is critically important for your success and the success of your major initiatives. To confirm, if you were hired into your leadership role with the expectation that you would drive change, it will be easy for you to simply love your school or institution for what it might become. But if you don't also love it for what it is, you will be disrespecting those faculty who have worked hard in shaping it as it is now. Remember, too, that you can't implement ideas taken from other institutions without a critical review of their fit with your new school community and culture.

OUTCOMES

Don't assume you can dictate results. Leaders, especially academic leaders, allocate attention and set agendas. They have little say on outcomes.

It's true, your ability to set agendas is one of your most powerful weapons in the fight for progress and change that matters. That power also comes with responsibilities. When you set an agenda – for meetings, for an academic year – it is presumed that you will stick with it, deviating only in the most extreme circumstances. And it is presumed that you will add further agendas only to the extent they will not undermine or diminish energy allocated to those previously set.

PECCADILLOS

Don't begrudge your faculty and staff their own personal peccadillos. We are all entitled to have at least one.

We each have areas of weakness. Dignified living is not about eliminating all our weaknesses, but doing our best to continually improve where and how we might. There is much to be gained from having a generous orientation to weaknesses in others. Celebrate what is good and beautiful, and accept that, for each of us, movement through life necessarily comes with inbuilt challenges, some greater, some lesser.

POLITICS

Don't be drawn into political argument, even while you continually strengthen your ability to act with political deftness.

Yes, being an academic leader certainly requires political deftness. And if you are in a senior leadership role within a public university, it may require interaction with political figures at regional and state levels, an interaction that may at times be exceptionally challenging. Regardless of your situation vis-à-vis politicians, always be cautious near overtly political issues. In maintaining good relationships with individuals across the political spectrum, you will help to safeguard resources and avoid undue pressures. That said, 21st-century academic leaders are expected to support the right of those who are vulnerable to be treated with dignity and respect, and to stand up for the values of inclusion, equity and diversity. Remember that any opportunity to affirm those values, especially during moments of social crisis, is an obligation in disguise. Of course, what words you use to describe your efforts may well differ if your institution is beholden to a state legislature that has been launching or is threatening to launch ideological assaults on diversity and inclusion priorities. (See, also, "Racism.")

POST-HIRE

Don't assume that it is unnecessary to share words of praise for your new faculty or leaders after they are hired. People like to feel wanted and valued, and appreciate receiving attention from their supervisor far beyond the time they join a community.

It is very easy to forget that individuals you have helped to bring with open arms into your fold need ongoing support and validation. You have an opportunity to not only ensure individuals feel entirely welcome when they join your school, but that they continually feel valued. Understand it doesn't take much to enable them to feel so. An email reaching out to congratulate them on an accomplishment or to check into how they are doing can go a long way to making them feel valued. (See, also, "Gestures.")

PRESENCE

Don't think that because you can't attend an entire faculty presentation or program that you shouldn't attend at all. Even slipping in to catch the first ten minutes will be appreciated if it comes from a spirit of care.

It is important that you make an effort to support faculty and staff as you can. The fact that you can't attend a full presentation or performance shouldn't keep you from showing up. It will typically mean the world to your faculty and staff that you have done what you can to publicly support them. And be mindful when you do choose to attend a full program or event that it doesn't set up a pattern that could be interpreted as a preference for one area or group of faculty over another.

PRESIDENT — FOR PROVOSTS AND DEANS

Don't pass up any opportunity to build a trusting relationship with your president, and to help your president look good, especially around donors and members of the board of trustees. It seems obvious, but bears restating: the success of your president impacts your own, and vice versa.

The reality is that the contemporary university or college president necessarily has (and needs) a large ego. (How else would one assume they have the ability to do a job that is close to impossible, given the presence of innumerable competing interests and incompatible priorities?) Daily, your president will face exceptional pressures. Whenever you have a chance, share your support and thanks for their leadership. They won't forget your show of support. They need public affirmation, not only for their own well-being but also for the perceived vitality and integrity of the institution.

PROBLEM SOLVING

Don't try to solve every problem within your sphere. Rather, slowly build a culture and community where people are empowered to address their own problems. Allow and enable internal leaders to develop as problem solvers.

There are few things that will waste your time more than becoming known as the person who solves other people's problems. Yes, some problems are so challenging that faculty leaders will be compelled to approach you and should approach you for guidance and resolution. But, to the fullest extent possible, if individuals approach you with problems, ask for their thoughts on possible solutions. Make it clear that you expect others to do their fair share in addressing issues as they arise. (See, also, "Burdens" and "Judiciousness.")

PROCESS

Don't ignore process. The vast majority of faculty life is about process, and the greatest misfortunes befall academic leaders who fail to follow process.

This point cannot be overstated. The most common pitfall for academic leaders is their failure (even briefly) to follow process. Faculty feel and understand that they don't have much in their control. They do, however, feel control around process. They cherish their understanding of processes and typically expect that they will be followed to the letter. This is to say, they feel deep ownership and investment in process. Undermine it at your peril. (See, also, "Promotion and Tenure.")

PROMISES

Don't break promises made to your faculty, however large or small. If you have promised to end a meeting at three o'clock, think twice before going a minute longer.*

It is vital that you keep all your promises, large and small. Few things are more central to a good working relationship with your faculty and staff than your habit of keeping your word. And your word will most often be shared regarding small matters. Doing what you said you would – whether a quick follow-up on a matter or further consideration of an issue – will go a long way to further strengthen your reputation as a competent and trustworthy leader. (See, also, "Respect.")

PROMOTION AND TENURE

Don't fail to follow to the letter faculty handbook guidelines relating to promotion and tenure.

No undertaking is more important within the academy than supporting faculty development and ensuring a fair process in faculty evaluation. There are remarkably few things that faculty truly have in their control. One thing they rely on is that the stated processes will be followed to the letter, especially as related to their position within the institution. The greatest betrayal for any faculty member is that they have been treated unfairly given faculty handbook guidelines. Remain a champion of fairness and process, and a leading advocate for faculty success. (See, also, "Process.")

PROVOST – FOR DEANS

Don't pass on opportunities to help your provost succeed. That is both the right and prudent thing to do. Your provost can support (or undermine) you and your school in more ways than you imagine.

There are few positions that have as great authority with as little power as a provost. Consider, the provost is stuck between a president who leads an institution and deans who lead their respective schools. What provosts lead is process, and a number of initiatives that the president has charged them with (whether a painful task such as leading decision-making on weather-related campus closures, or a complex task such as overseeing the development of a strategic plan). Their work is typically thankless and complex. Treat them with respect. And yes, they can undermine your success in more ways than you can imagine.

QUESTIONS

Don't assume you alone can (or should) figure out the puzzles you face. Your job very often is to make sure the right questions have been asked and to learn the answer.

There are few skills of greater worth in leadership than the skill of asking the right questions. Hone that skill as best you can. And make it a habit to close a session of investigation with the pointed question, "Is there anything else we're not considering?" You'll be surprised how often that simple question will yield additional and important insight. (See, also, "Listening" and "Problems.")

RACISM

Don't overlook your biases towards others. Consider and walk towards those biases, and continually build your network of friends to include others not like you.

Beyond undertaking a personal journey towards anti-racism, what can you as an academic leader be expected to do in relation to something so embedded in society, something that has become a core part of the culture over multiple generations? Well, if you belong to an institution that believes in inclusion and diversity, you and your community have every right to speak up and out for the right of all to be treated with dignity and respect. That, of course, is made more difficult if your institution happens to be beholden to a state legislature that is launching ideological attacks against racial equity and inclusion efforts. Racism is not aberrational but ordinary. You have the chance to push back against it, both personally and institutionally. You have the chance to become an ally of those who would advance a society that is equitable. Remember, you as a leader are especially responsible for the most vulnerable. You can make a difference, and should. (See, also, "Politics.")

REBUKE

Don't rebuke faculty members in public. They won't easily forgive you for a public scolding.*

It might be the smallest of things, a quick aside during a meeting that shoots down a faculty member's idea or rebukes someone in light of a questionable action or comment. If you presume that each of your faculty and staff is sensitive to criticism, and you endeavor to treat them as you would wish to be treated, you will avoid these sorts of mistakes. If you need to point out a misstep, do it in private. Make no doubt about it; many of your faculty do not believe they have to uphold the level of integrity that you, as a more senior academic leader, do. Which is to say, they hold you and your behavior to a higher standard. Don't disappoint them.

RISK-TAKING

Don't simply refine processes and elevate established projects and programs. Experiment and take risks, judiciously, as you can.

Few truly innovative enterprises and noteworthy changes happen without significant risk-taking. Unfortunately (or fortunately), academic leaders differ in their comfort with taking risks. If you are by temperament on the cautious side, begin by supporting those faculty who would take calculated risks. Slowly, you will develop your own comfort in taking risks. And, yes, it is hard to learn both how to be comfortable with taking risks and also how to perceive which risks are truly worthy of effort. Practice, and you will build that capacity and skill.

SECOND CHANCES

Don't neglect to give second chances to all: faculty, students, and staff. Except, of course, when the offense is so grave as to be cause for dismissal.

Why is it so important to give people second chances? Well, for starters, to be human is to be imperfect. And to live in the 21st century and be working within a higher education institution is to be not infrequently overwhelmed by the scope and pace of ongoing change. Just as you will want a second chance when you screw up on something big (and you will), extend that courtesy to others. That humane and generous gesture will make a big difference and won't be easily forgotten.

SEXISM

Don't be reluctant to actively fight sexism in the workplace. Regardless of your gender, stand up for change.

Though perhaps too obvious to warrant repetition, the fact is that sexism is not only housed within much speech and action but also exists perniciously in systems. Keep an eye on such things as the salary levels of your faculty and staff, being on the lookout for differences in pay between employees of different genders. Such differences can creep in without your or anyone's awareness. Likewise, keep an eye out for any possible differences in the assignment of benefits, from scholarship release time to the awarding of promotions, stipends, or school-wide awards.

SMALL THINGS

Don't ignore the small things. Much of effective leadership comes from doing ordinary things well. From making honest promises, starting and ending meetings on time, and asking others rather than promoting your own ideas.

This is not to say that your job doesn't require you to keep an eye on the big picture and make significant decisions about complex and large issues. It does, and that goes doubly if you are a provost or dean. But it is your ability to do ordinary things well which will keep your meetings efficient and successful, your working relationships strong, and your important initiatives in forward motion.

SOCIAL MEDIA

Don't embrace it overmuch. With few exceptions, social media in the workplace results in more difficulties than benefits.

You may be aware of professional and personal boundaries, but social media is not. Yes, there are multiple advantages to you being highly visible in ways that matter to your students, alumni, or donors. But unless you have professional support for social media – that is to say, a staff member who helps you post and is skilled in navigating potential issues – you may well trip up or have someone gravely misinterpret a statement or image of yours, or (and this is no small thing) be left with no time at the transition points in your day, moments when you might otherwise be reflecting, daydreaming, scheming, or even recharging. Regarding misinterpretation, understand that the medium is no match for people's imaginations. Yes, social media is of great value to your school's programming and profile. But when it comes to you personally, treat it with the caution it deserves.

SOLITUDE

Don't be afraid to drop work at critical junctures to take a walk in nature and truly be alone. Few things can aid perspective and self-knowledge as well a good stretch of solitude.

The above statement intentionally advances the importance of two simultaneous things: walking in nature and truly being alone. As researchers have continually found, a walk in nature – one in which the person is naturally observing things both right and left – does wonders to help the brain integrate ideas. And being alone in that endeavor allows you to move and interact with your environment at exactly the pace that feels right to you at the time. Of course, if you live in a large city, your challenge will be to become familiar with and gain access to parks or gardens in your area. In all likelihood, there is some way for you to be in nature near where you work and live. (See, also, "Time Outs.")

SOLUTIONS

Don't look for perfect solutions. As an academic leader, you are more often dealing with personalities and relationships than accounting.

Although you may wish it otherwise, you will often have to navigate problems stemming from the messiness of personalities and relationships. Whether deciding how to help two faculty who are stepping on each other's toes rebuild a working relationship, or how to navigate a complex situation with a disgruntled student or would-be donor, your need will be not to find a perfect solution – there likely won't be one – but to find a workable solution. Be clear with all about the goal you are pursuing, and (where possible) invite the involved individuals into the work of shaping a solution. (See, also, "Choices.")

STRATEGIC PLANNING

Don't ignore the benefits and challenges of strategic planning. It's easy to assume that since you've gotten people on board during the planning phase the implementation phase will go smoothly. It won't if there is insufficient oversight. During all stages, ensure that work is transparent, well communicated, and broadly involves your community.

An academic community can be greatly energized when the task of building a strategic plan engages all key constituents. And broad ownership of a plan ensures it has a greater chance of surviving any changes to the university's senior leadership. Paying careful attention at the planning stages is, however, insufficient. While a plan's formation process might be energizing, the hard work of managing and monitoring its implementation is as unsatisfying as it is necessary. Proud of having created a good strategic plan, many institutions falter during the unrewarding work of implementing it. On top of that, many institutions find that the size and speed of changes in the surrounding environment mean that carefully crafted goals and foundational assumptions are quickly made irrelevant. What is to be done? Ultimately, the soundest investment is ensuring shared ownership, maintaining transparency and communication, and consistently affirming that the institution will move on from one or more parts of a strategic plan if they become irrelevant.

STUDENT-CENTERED

Don't think that just because an institution is student-centered that it can't (and shouldn't) also be faculty- and staff-centered. If you put at the center of your work faculty and staff who put students and disciplinary excellence at the center of their work, you will be doing well.

It is not coincidental that the idea of "student-centered" grew alongside the rise in college tuition rates. Indeed, given the exorbitant amounts that most institutions charge students (or, more commonly, their parents), it is not surprising that universities and colleges are doing all they can to appeal to potential students. There is a simple way in which you can honor what is best about the "student-centered" concept without losing sight of one of your greatest responsibilities, namely, the support for and success of your faculty and staff. Put at the center of your life the work of hiring and supporting faculty and staff who put at the center of their lives students, their own work and development, and your community. To confirm, the best of your faculty will always be individuals who are oriented to students' and their own ongoing development. As bell hooks helpfully explained regarding authentic learning and teaching, "Engaged pedagogy does not seek simply to empower students. Any classroom that employs a holistic model of learning will also be a place where teachers grow and are empowered by the process."

STUDENTS, CONTEMPORARY

Don't assume their values and outlook align with yours or those of your faculty. Students have a newfound willingness to question, probe, and assert contrary opinions to those in positions of authority. Engage them whenever you can, understanding there are good reasons for their increased sensitivities.

As you've likely noticed, we are living through a global pandemic, a climate crisis, an opioid epidemic, a global refugee crisis, a global crisis in food security, and an era of continuing inequity and civil unrest amid political upheaval. Put differently, we are living in an age of trauma, an age when many have lost their ability to count on the stability of the planet, and have lost their faith in authority and progress. It should not be surprising then that young people are largely disinterested in viewing their elders with admiration and respect. In many ways, we have been failing the next generation. What can you, as an academic leader, do? For one, encourage your internal leaders and faculty to engage with students, inviting them into decision-making regarding those things where their input could prove insightful (i.e., most things). Just as importantly, model engagement and openness by ensuring that students have a voice in your own work – whether through a student council or the like. As many academic leaders have found, you will often be surprised by students' insights, insights that seem far beyond their years and experience. Navigating this anti-establishment era calmly will likely be one of the most difficult challenges you face. There is no easy way forward. What is vital is that your entire community sense and feel they are in this work together.

SUFFERING

Don't pass up an opportunity to reach out to faculty and staff who are suffering (or have loved ones who are). Be patient with them; it is difficult to remain level-headed in the face of pain.

If you oversee a larger department or school, it is very likely that at any given time, you will have at least one faculty or staff member who is battling cancer, or dealing with a major loss, or supporting a close family member who is navigating personal difficulty. Make it a habit to reach out to individuals in such circumstances with a message of support. And ensure that your assistant (if you have one) knows to keep you in the loop when news of personal difficulty surfaces. Unless the involved individual requests otherwise, keep the issues you become aware of strictly confidential. Act in a way that shows care and kindness.

SUPERSTAR FACULTY

Don't grumble day after day at the drama surrounding a superstar faculty member. It will be much easier and will save friction if you quietly help settle issues that they leave behind.*

Yes, the challenges associated with one or more of your superstar faculty may relate to a constitutional defect. If so (and you choose to keep them), no amount of grumbling or demanding will cure it. What is the best you can do? Steer those faculty away from tasks and areas where you know they will especially cause disruption.

TECHNOLOGY, NEW

Don't fail to keep an eye on true costs. While new technology can fix some problems and increase some efficiencies, it invariably causes new problems. Approach with mild skepticism.

With their ever-increasing complexities of operation, 21st-century higher education institutions are understandably enticed by promises that new technology will solve many problems. Whether related to decreasing costs, improving some important functionality related to your operations, increasing data governance and security, strengthening the success of your students and/or employees, or the like, newly available technological tools will promise much. But make no mistake, their implementation will come with unexpected costs. Always plan on needing more money and allocating more support time than is advertised as needed for training and upkeep. And if there's one thing that the past few decades have taught us, it is that technological aids for productivity often come at the cost of increasing people's workdays, reducing autonomy, and even increasing surveillance capacities. The bottom line? In acquiring new technology, you will inevitably find that you have not so much gotten rid of problems as replaced them with new ones. In a best-case scenario, the replacement represents an upgrade, your new problems being of a lesser sort than the old ones.

TIME

Don't forget to jealously guard your time, especially your time with family and loved ones. As Jane Kenyon advised, protect your time, feed your inner life.

Though it's hard to find relevant research, one can't help but suspect that the number of senior academic leaders who have divorced or are in the process of divorcing is likely higher than the norm within academia. The reason for the suspicion is straightforward: individuals who have advanced to a high position within academia have usually been aggressively focused on their professional success and development. Such focus – critical to advancement – typically comes at the cost of personal relationships. If this sounds familiar to you, do all you can to ensure that your greatest energies and creativity aren't only focused on your work. Your family and partner or spouse (if you have one) deserve the full you as well. So importantly, your ability to succeed long-term will be buoyed by the presence of strong personal relationships. It's unlikely that any academic leaders have approached the end of their careers wishing they had spent more time at work.

TIMEOUTS – FOR PROVOSTS AND DEANS

Don't ever disregard the feeling when it arises that you need some time out – whether from an argument or project. You won't be missed much if you take a little time away, and you will return all the better able to tackle that which is difficult.

Perhaps few things are as characteristic of a seasoned academic leader as the ability to perceive when time away from a problem or people is vital and to willingly take that time away. Yes, ongoing emergencies will demand your attention. But there will always be emergencies. While you have a responsibility to succeed in the present moment, you have a still greater responsibility to succeed long term. When you sense your decision-making would be stronger if you took some brief time off to gain further perspective, do so. Your well-being and overall success will be strengthened. Put differently; foresters know that how hard you are sawing is less important than how sharp your saw is. Take time to sharpen your saw when it is dull. (See, also, "Executive Assistant" and "Solitude.")

UNCOMMON OPPORTUNITIES

Don't spend equal energy on all large opportunities. They are not equally important.

As many academic leaders have found, each year brings with it at least two or three extraordinary decision points, opportunities when your action will make an unusually large impact on your community. Just knowing that such decision points exist will go a good way to helping you be alert and prepared. Keep an eye out for them. Your success as a leader depends on your ability to spot those opportunities and act on them.

WARMTH

Don't rush headlong into your meetings in such a hurry that you fail to warmly welcome your faculty. Such disregard can easily cast a shadow.*

You may have every reason to quickly begin a meeting. For example, the meeting's tasks might be huge, requiring more time than what is available. However, there are few investments with greater payback than taking time to warmly greet others. It may be a small gesture, and may not take more than fifteen seconds, but it will set the meeting's tone. Even more importantly, it will reinforce to your faculty and staff your community's values and way of doing business. (See, also, "Gestures" and "Kindness.")

WORDS

Don't pay as much attention to words as you do to the speaker. As Charles Péguy helpfully explained, a word or idea is not the same with one individual as it is with another. One might pull it out of her jacket while another tears it from his gut.

There are two relatively complex issues here. The first is the now well-known fact that words are of secondary importance in human communication. As has repeatedly been shown, when we talk with each other, our communication is primarily non-verbal; we infer meaning by paying less attention to spoken words and more attention to gestures and body language, tone of voice, and facial expressions. The second issue here is that even if two people use the same tone, their words can differ greatly in meaning. If a very introverted faculty member thanks you for something, pay attention. Those words of thanks likely came from much consideration. Likewise, if introverted staff members speak up with a concern at a meeting, make no mistake that it is of great importance to them. Ignore that concern at your peril.

WORK

Don't make work your life. Have a life when you leave campus at day's end.

Few things will hollow you out faster than a long succession of days in which your focus is singularly on your work. If you don't have a partner or family to take your attention at day's end, find and pursue a hobby. As many have discovered the hard way, it is vitally important for you to gain meaning from more than just your job. As rich and challenging as your job may be, it alone cannot nurture your soul and support your long-term well-being.

YESTERDAY

Don't respond to an angry email or phone call without letting an evening pass. By all means, indicate that you are considering the message. But then give it time. After a night's rest, you will be able to reshape the reply you had rashly wished to send yesterday.

Little further needs to be said. No one has ever wished they had shared an angry retort more quickly than they did. Though it doesn't appear in your job description, you can be certain that among your responsibilities are "being a peacekeeper" and "being the most mature person in the room." (See, also, "Email.")